THE EPPE RESEARCH TEAM
PRINCIPAL INVESTIGATORS
Professor Kathy Sylva
Department of Educational Studies, University of Oxford

Professor Edward Melhuish
Institute for the Study of Children, Families and Social Issues, Birkbeck, University of London

Professor Pam Sammons
Institute of Education, University of London

Professor Iram Siraj-Blatchford
Institute of Education, University of London

Research Co-ordinator
Brenda Taggart
Institute of Education, University of London

Acknowledgements

This research was supported by a grant from the UK Department of Education and Skills to the London Institute of Education. We would like to acknowledge the following, all of whom deserve our thanks. Firstly, all the pre-school staff, children and parents who participated in the research. Secondly our Research Officers: Anne Dobson, Marj Jeavons, Katie Lewis, Maria Morahan, Sharon Sadler and Lidia Trojanowska. Finally, our colleagues who contributed to the development of this publication: Liz Brooker, Paul Colman, Debby Cryer, Bernadette Duffy, Julie Fisher, Lynn Kennington and John Siraj-Blatchford.

Contents

Literacy Items 1-6

Mathematics Items 1-4

Science and Environment Items 1-5

Foreword

It gives me great pleasure to write a foreword to the English Extension to the Early Childhood Environment Rating Scale- Revised (ECERS-R). In planning for the use of the ECERS-R in their research on the Effective Provision of Pre-school Education (EPPE) Project, the authors of the English Extension anticipated the need to expand several of the ECERS items into subscales. These additional subscales were necessary in order to assess areas of emphasis in the English Curriculum Guidance for the Foundation State (3-5+). Before they began work on the Extension, they asked for our advice and ideas, which we were happy to give.

The authors of the English Extension are highly respected experts in the Early Childhood field. They are also valued colleagues of ours, and long time users of the ECERS. At every step of the way, they have shared their work with us and with many others who use the ECERS for research in different countries. The resulting English Extension, which consists of four curricular subscales, is completely in keeping with both the formal aspects and the educational philosophy of the ECERS. The EPPE Project researchers have used the English Extension along with the ECERS-R, and consider the two assessment instruments to be complementary.

I wish to commend the authors of the English Extension on their very careful work and look forward to seeing it in print. I believe it will prove useful in programme assessment in England and beyond.

Professor Thelma Harms
University of North Carolina, Chapel Hill.

Lead author of *Early Childhood Environment Rating Scale – Revised.*
(Harms, Cryer and Clifford, 1998)

Introduction to the ECERS-E

The Early Childhood Environment Rating Scale (Harms, Clifford and Cryer, 1998) is an imaginative and sturdy tool for research, self-audit and inspection. It has been used in more than twenty countries – from Singapore to Germany to Chile. Those who use it in countries outside the US often do little more than translate the instrument into the national language, making minor modifications to vocabulary or to types of equipment. This is what has been done in Germany (Tietze, 1996), in the United Kingdom (Sylva et al, 1999) and in Portugal (Bairrao, 1996). Elsewhere, as in *Tamil Nadu* in India, researchers such as Swaminathan (2000) have used the ECERS as a conceptual template on which to build a very different assessment system to suit environments and practices which are far removed from the American Early Childhood Settings in which ECERS was first developed.

In England, the ECERS-R has been found to be appropriate to statutory, private and voluntary settings. It has been used successfully in research (Melhuish 1994; Sylva et al. 1999) and to improve practice through self-audit (Siraj-Blatchford, 2002a,b). However, the ECERS-R was developed in the 1980s, based broadly on notions of Developmentally Appropriate Practice (DAP). It adopts a light touch to assessing provision for developing children's emerging literacy, numeracy and scientific thinking. It is also light on assessing provision aimed at cultural and intellectual diversity in the setting. The Early Childhood Environment Rating Scale – Extension (ECERS-E) was developed to supplement the ECERS-R by a team of researchers at the Institute of Education, University of London. ECERS-E reflects the English National Early Childhood Curriculum Curriculum Guidance for the Foundation Stage (QCA 2000) as well as the changing notions of Developmentally Appropriate Practice.

Four new sub-scales have been devised for the ECERS-E: Literacy, Mathematics, Science, and Diversity. Items in these sub-scales assess the quality of curricular provision, including pedagogy, in these domains aimed at fostering children's academic development (Sammons et al 2002).

The ECERS-E has been piloted extensively in a variety of settings for predictive validity (Sylva AERA 2001). A study of 3,000 children in Britain (The Effective Provision of Pre-School Education (EPPE) Project, Institute of Education, University of London) has shown that assessments of their Early Childhood Settings made on the ECERS-E are better predictors of children's intellectual and language progress (3-5 years) than were assessments on the same settings using the ECERS-R. This validation came from a national study carried out in England to explore the relationship between the quality of pre-school measured by the Early Childhood Environment Rating Scale-Revised (ECERS-R) and the developmental progress of more than

3,000 pre-school children. This study is part of the Effective Provision of Pre-school Education (EPPE) project funded by the UK government. The study follows the development of children between entry to pre-school at the age of 3 and entry to school at age 5 years. The predictive validity of the ECERS-R was compared to this extension (ECERS-E) relying on the same format but with more detailed assessment of the 'curricular environment' which is specified in the *English Foundation Stage Curriculum Guidance*, QCA (2000). Scores on the total ECERS-R were not related to cognitive progress over the two year period but the scores on one of its subscales 'Social Interaction' were positively related to increases in children's **independence** and **cooperation.** For academic development, however, the ECERS-E was significantly related to progress in children's **language**, **non-verbal reasoning**, **number skills**, and **pre-reading skills**. We suggest that quality is not a universal concept but depends on national priorities. If academic achievement is valued at the start of school, then the ECERS-E is a good predictor of readiness for school. But if social outcomes are valued, then the social interaction scale on the ECERS-R may be a better predictor of readiness.

However, we believe both are equally important and therefore recommend that the scales should be used together. ECERS-R is available from Teachers College Press (see Appendix C for ordering information for both this and other EPPE publications).

How to use the ECERS-E rating scale

Before using the scale

Before using the ECERS-E scale as either a self-assessment tool (see next section) or a research instrument, it is strongly recommended that the user has some familiarity with the ECERS-R scale. The Teachers College Press have produced a range of materials to accompany the scales that have been developed for training purposes. These include video extracts and advice on making judgements. These materials can be used for both group and self-instruction. After viewing the training package, users will need to conduct several 'trial' observations in order to familiarise themselves with the content of the items included in the scale. This cannot be done on one observation. Using the scales demands a high degree of understanding about not only the content of the scales but about making sense of what is being observed. In many cases information to complete the scales cannot be readily observed and the user may need to question centre staff sensitively about their practices. Any user therefore needs to be familiar with the content of the scales and also to be confident in probing for additional information beyond that which is observed.

Before using the scales, users should note that it is also strongly recommended that the observer have some external validation conducted on their judgements. This could be done by a colleague or outsider as a measure of inter-rater reliability. This may need to be arranged before the period of observations to ensure that the inter-rater will be available.

Administering the scale

Preparing for the observation

1　Sufficient time should be put aside to conduct the observations. One half day is recommended. Make sure that the time set aside allow for enough time to talk to staff without children present (usually at the end of the observation) so that you can ask any additional questions. It is recommended that you allow approximately fifteen minutes to do this.

2　The room or area in which the observations take place should be clearly defined i.e. is it just the room/provision for 3 year olds which is going to be observed or a whole centre?

3　Before beginning the observation ensure you have completed as much of the identifying information as possible i.e. names of centre, age group observed etc.

4　Spend sometime before the observations orientating yourself to the centre and its geography. It is a good idea to find out from the staff what programme of activities is planned during the period of the observation.

5   If you need to see additional paperwork to assist you in making a judgement such as planning documents, make sure that the staff know you are going to ask to see (or be given copies) of these. Allow sufficient time for staff to get these for you.

6   Make sure that you are clear about the value placed on some of the terms used throughout the scale i.e. 'a few' (Environmental print 3.1) suggests a limited number, probably no more than 5, however 'many' (same item 5.1) suggests an amount over 10. Clear distinctions (% value) should be made between 'few', 'some', 'many', 'variety', 'most', 'sometimes' and agreed by the observer and inter-rater. In this context 'easily accessible' (i.e. books and literacy areas) means that children can reach and use materials easily, not necessarily that every child has to have access at all times. Similarly the term 'staff' refers to all adults who have direct contact with children.

Conducting the observation

1   The items do not have to be administered in the order they appear in the booklet. If a cooking activity is taking place you may decide to score this immediately and then come back to other items later on. Some items may be scored more easily than others. Resources for instance are easier to observe.

2   Only score an item after you have allowed sufficient time to make a reasoned judgement. This is particularly important for items which demand observing the interactions between adult/child or child/child. You need to be sure that what you are observing is representative of the practices as a whole.

3   Take care not to interrupt the activities being observed. The observer should be a 'fly on the wall' and should avoid interacting with the children or staff. It is important to be as unobtrusive as possible and to remain neutral in you actions, expressions and reply to questions.

4   If you are not sure about something make detailed notes on your scoring sheet and ensure that these are clear enough for you to follow when you come back to them at the end of the observation. This is particularly important if you are using the scales for self-evaluation and plan to give feedback to others on your observations.

5   Make sure you score all items at the time of the observation. It is very difficult to record scores away from the setting.

6   A new score sheet should be used for each observation (permission to photocopy score sheets ONLY is granted) and you should make sure that the scoring is both legible and photocopiable. It is recommended that you use a pencil and have a rubber with you to amend scoring as you work.

Scoring the scales

THIS CAN ONLY BE DONE ONCE THE OBSERVER IS FAMILIAR WITH THE SCALE.

1. Read the items carefully, as judgements have to be made exactly in accordance with the instructions given.
2. Scores must reflect the observed practice and not some future plan the centre may have told you about.
3. The scale measures from 1 to 7 with 1 = inadequate, 3 = minimal 5 = good and 7 = excellent.
4. The observation should always start with 1 and be worked though systematically.
5. A rating of 1 must be given if **any** indicator in section 1 is scored YES.
6. A rating of 2 is given when **all** indicators under 1 are scored NO and at least half of the indicators under 3 are scored YES.
7. A rating of 3 is given when **all** indicators under 1 scored NO and all indictors under 3 are scored YES.
8. A rating of 4 is given when **all** indicators under 3 are met and at least half of the indicators under 5 are scored YES.
9. A rating of 5 is given when **all** indicators under 5 are scored YES.
10. A rating of 6 is given when **all** indicators under 5 are met and at least half of the indicators under 7 are scored YES.
11. A rating of 7 is given when **all** indicators under 7 are scored YES.
12. A score of NA (Not Applicable) may only be given for indicators or for entire items when this scale is omitted i.e. on maths and science activities where a choice of observed activities is allowed.
13. To calculate average subscale scores, sum the scores for each item in the sub-scale and divide by the number of items scored. The total mean scale score is the sum of all item scores for the entire scale divided by the number of items scored.

N.B. These administrative notes are based on the ECERS-R guidance. We are grateful to the Chapel Hill Team for their assistance in helping us write our guidance notes.

Using ECERS as a self assessment and improvement tool at centre level

Since the publication of the Effective Provision of Pre-School Education (EPPE) Technical Papers which relate quality, as measured by ECERS-R and ECERS-E, with child cognitive and social developmental outcomes, we have been inundated with requests for the ECERS-E document (which was particularly significant for cognitive outcomes – see Introduction) not only within the UK but from around the world. Although we have provided copies of the ECERS-E and given the details of where to purchase ECERS-R in response to these requests, we have been concerned about how this rating scale is used. We have asked people what they have wanted the scale for and most have replied that they want to use it in some way in their early childhood or Foundation Stage settings, or as a research instrument.

As a team we have discussed what it means for people to use the scales when they haven't been trained to do so. We have been concerned about their use in settings where the general professional training of the staff may be limited. In such circumstances we are sure that critical but constructive support will be needed. We have also been concerned about the lack of external validation, which means that settings can rate themselves as good, excellent, or in need of further development but where there is no real comparative measure.

It was for these reasons that one of us used the ECERS-R and ECERS-E as part of the Early Excellence Evaluations of two centres over a period of two to three years (Siraj-Blatchford, 2002a and 2002b). With the support of the heads and senior teachers, the ECERS were used as a self-development tool by both centres. The centres that trialled this application of the instruments were the Gamesley Early Excellence Centre in Derbyshire and the Thomas Coram and Coram Parents' Early Excellence Centre in London.

All staff were initially provided with a full day's training on what is meant by 'quality', the culturally specific aspects of it, as well as what we consider are some universal aspects e.g. treating children with respect, not harming or smacking children. Then the staff were introduced to the ECERS-R and the ECERS-E. The staff were asked to systematically assess the ratings from the scale on adults and children in different centres shown on video working together. They were given time to compare and discuss their judgements. The training materials used are produced by Teachers College Press, and the training was delivered by a trained researcher/user of the scale. The staff were then asked to trial two of the scales for themselves working in pairs and to report back their findings, their agreements and disagreements, during a follow-up half day training session.

During the two years, the staff regularly reported on their discussions and progress with the scales. They found it easier to begin by rating the less threatening subscales such as furnishings and display. From this they learnt that it was the discussions themselves that provided the most useful outcome. These discussions led them to reach agreed meanings for good practice. The staff recommended that each rater should discuss their ratings, done independently but based on the same observations, immediately after the event and compare their ratings and discuss why it was that perceptions sometimes differed. As the staff developed in confidence in their rating and discussion they became more critical of their setting and their practices, and at times also more critical about aspects of the scales. All this was perceived as productive, as most of their observations led to positive actions. For instance at the Thomas Coram EEC, after rating their Language and Reasoning' subscale, they decided to take action as follows:

Within six months' to:

- provide in-service training for all staff on extending children's conversations, focusing on developing the use of open-ended questions.
- establish listening areas in the rooms used by children aged 3 – 5 yrs.

Within a year:

- the need is identified to order more dressing-up clothes and to increase the range and quality of the clothes for socio-dramatic play.

Similarly at the Gamesley EEC after rating the ECERS-R sub-scale on Personal Care Routines, staff decided the following on the item 'greetings and departures':

Staff felt the organisation of the nursery greeting the parents and children was very good on the whole but some of the staff felt the departure in the afternoon meant that some children missed out on the important story session. The staff also felt there wasn't enough time to talk or share information with the parents. *All very rushed.* Parents also have to hunt for their children, as each nursery officer went into a different room for small group/story time. There was intense discussion amongst the staff about ways in which they could improve departure time.

Action taken:
The time of arrival and departure time for children who attended nursery in the afternoon was changed. The session used to start at 12.45pm and finish at 3.15pm. Now, instead of going into small groups for story time, all the nursery groups join together for a large group story. The staff, on a rota basis, read the story. Parents now collect their children from this group. This helps parents know where their children are and gives the nursery officers who are not reading the story time to share information with parents to about their child.

Impact:
The story sessions are no longer interrupted and there are opportunities for staff and parents to discuss matters regarding about their children.

In both these centres, examples from the ECERS-R and E were documented and discussed. Actions were decided and taken. There was extensive monitoring of the changes made and the outcomes were recorded and revisited. This developmental work allowed staff to reflect, plan and monitor the children's welfare and learning, and for both centres it became an integral part of the ongoing centre development plans and policies.

After two years of such development, the centre heads agreed to take part in an external validation exercise where another trained researcher came into the centre, without any prior knowledge of it, and rated it for its environmental quality, using both the ECERS-R and E. Both centres scored an average of six on both scales, placing them between good and excellent on both. They are continuing to use the scales and are now also looking at ITERS (Infant and Toddler Environmental Rating Scale) to engage in self-assessment and the development of their practice with the children under three years old.

What has been learnt from this experience? Both the headteachers were interviewed as part of their annual evaluation and both had obviously taken the exercise very seriously. When asked why they undertook this in their centre, they replied:

'It's about being brave enough to be objective, it's about being self-critical and hard on yourself' Bernadette Duffy, Head of Thomas Coram and Coram Parents' Early Excellence Centre.

'The discussion process is the best, we got quite high scores but we could be doing better than even what's measured, we as staff are not entirely happy with this and feel we could go further' Lynn Kennington, Head Gamesley Early Excellence Centre.

Clearly, ECERS can be used effectively as a self-assessment and improvement tool at pre-school centre or reception class level (first year of compulsory schooling) as long as the following criteria are met:

- Rigorous training is provided on both the quality criteria (definitions and cultural variations) and on the use and the role of the scales.
- It is recognised that an exercise of this nature requires a critical mass of reflective practitioners within the setting.
- That a critical friend supports the initiative (an insider e.g. local authority adviser or a representative from Higher Education. In the cases of Gamesley and Thomas Coram cited above, their external evaluator also acted as critical friend).
- There is a willingness to undergo external validation ('blind' assessment by a trained, reliable assessor).

We are grateful to the staff and the head teachers of both Gamesley and Thomas Coram EECs for their time and efforts in using ECERS and in helping us to understand how it can best be used by centres as a self-assessment tool.

Item	Inadequate		Minimal		Good		Excellent
	1	2	3	4	5	6	7

Literacy
Item 1. 'Environmental print': Letters and words

1.1 No pictures with printed labels accompanying them are visible to the children.

1.2 Attention is not drawn to letters or words outside of books.

3.1 A few labelled pictures are present and visible (may be above eye level but a child can see it easily).

3.2 Children see some printed words, such as labels on shelves or their own names on their coat pegs or paintings.

3.3 Printed words are prominently displayed e.g. 'welcome' on the door, or 'wash your hands'.

5.1 Many labelled pictures are on view (may be above eye level but a child can see it easily).

5.2 Children are encouraged to recognise printed words on everyday objects such as juice cans, food packaging, carrier bags.**

5.3 Children are encouraged to recognise letters in their own names.**

7.1 Discussion of environmental print takes place and often relates to objects the children bring to the centre.

7.2 There is discussion of the relationship between the spoken and the printed word.

7.3 Children are encouraged to recognise letters and words in the environment, e.g. in labels and words on posters.

Note**= If you do not observe children's attention being drawn to printed words (such as name-mats and labels) ask a 'prompt' question such as 'Do you draw attention to printed words?'

Item	Inadequate		Minimal		Good		Excellent
	1	2	3	4	5	6	7

Item 2. Book and literacy areas

1.1 If present, books are *unattractive and not of a suitable age level.

3.1 Some books of different kinds are available.

3.2 An easily accessible area of the room is set aside for books.

5.1 There is a variety of books, some picture books, many with text, and at a variety of levels to cater for different skills and interests.

5.2 Children regularly use the book area.

7.1 Book area is comfortable (rug and cushions or comfortable seating) and filled with a wide range of books at many levels of complexity.

7.2 Adults encourage children to use books and direct them to the book area.

7.3 Books are included in learning areas outside of the book corner.

Note* = this refers to the books themselves and not the way in which they are displayed.

Item	Inadequate		Minimal		Good		Excellent
	1	2	3	4	5	6	7

Item 3. Adult reading with the children

1.1 Adults rarely read to the children.

3.1 An adult reads with the children most days.

3.2 Children are encouraged to join in with repetitive words and phrases in the text.

5.1 Children take an active role in group reading during which the words and / or story are usually discussed.

5.2 Children are encouraged to conjecture about and comment on the text.

7.1 There is discussion about print and letters as well as content.

7.2 There is support material for the children to engage with the story by themselves e.g. tapes, flannel board, displays etc.

7.3 There is evidence of one to one reading with some children.

Item	Inadequate		Minimal		Good		Excellent
	1	2	3	4	5	6	7

Item 4. Sounds in words

1.1 Few or no nursery rhymes or poems are spoken or sung.	3.1 Rhymes are often spoken or sung by adults to children.	5.1 The rhyming components of songs and nursery rhymes are brought to the attention of children.	7.1 Attention is paid to syllabification of words through clapping games, jumping etc.
	3.2 Children are encouraged to speak and/or sing rhymes.	5.2 The initial sounds of alliterative in words and /or alliterative sentences are brought to the attention of children (e.g. Peter Piper picked a peck of pickled peppers).	7.2 Some attention is given to linking sounds to letters.

Item	Inadequate		Minimal		Good		Excellent
	1	2	3	4	5	6	7

Item 5. Emergent writing/mark making

1.1 There are no materials for children to engage in emergent writing.

1.2 There is no provision for children to observe what they say being written down.

3.1 Children have access to implements for writing such as pencils and felt tips.

3.2 Children have access to paper appropriate to a writing task, e.g. A4 or telephone pads.

5.1 A place in the setting is set aside for emergent writing.

5.2 Staff sometimes write down what children say.

7.1 As well as pencils and paper, the mark-making area has a theme to encourage children to 'write', e.g. an office.

7.2 The purpose of writing is emphasised, e.g. children are encouraged to 'write' and 'read', to communicate to others what they have produced.

7.3 Children's emergent writing is displayed for others to see.

Item	Inadequate		Minimal		Good		Excellent
	1	2	3	4	5	6	7

Item 6. Talking and Listening

1.1 Very little encouragement or opportunity for children to talk to adults.

1.2 Most verbal attention from adults is of a supervisory nature.

3.1 Some conversation between adults and children does occur.

3.2 Children are mostly permitted to talk amongst themselves. There is little adult intervention to extend conversation.

5.1 Interesting experiences are planned by adults and drawn upon to encourage talk and the sharing of ideas.

5.2 Children are encouraged to ask and answer questions.

5.3 Adults create one-to-one opportunities to talk with children by initiating conversations with individuals.

7.1 Adults provide scaffolding for children's conversations with them, that is, they accept and extend children's verbal contributions in conversation.

7.2 Children are often encouraged to talk in small groups and adults encourage their peers to listen to them.

Item	Inadequate		Minimal		Good		Excellent
	1	2	3	4	5	6	7

Mathematics – N.B. Items 1 and 2 MUST be assessed. After assessing Items 1 and 2 you may then select EITHER Item 3 or Item 4 for evidence. You may choose the Item that is most apparent during the observation. This mathematics subscale may require access to planning documents.

Item 1. Counting and the application of counting

1.1 Children rarely take part in routines where counting is used.

1.2 Very few resources are available to the children to encourage counting activities. (many are available e.g. conkers, shells, buttons, unifix cubes)

3.1 A few number routines such as counting, songs or rhymes are used with the children.

3.2 Numbers are named as part of routine activities.

3.3 Maths provision includes posters featuring numbers or counting books/games.

5.1 Number songs, rhymes, counting books and games are often used with the children.

5.2 Children are encouraged to count objects and to associate the spoken numbers with the numerical concepts. (e.g. six milk cartons for six children, two balls for two children)

5.3 Adults use both cardinal (1,2,3...) and ordinal (1st, 2nd, 3rd ..) numbers when working with the children.

7.1 All children are actively encouraged to take part in counting objects in a variety of contexts, e.g. role play, snack time, sharing lego.

7.2 Activities are planned which encourage one-to-one correspondence both inside and outside the setting.

7.3 Adults incorporate into their planning working with children on specific number activities, e.g. dice games, dominoes, matching numbers to numbers or numbers to pictures.

7.4 There is a well-equipped maths area with number games, objects and books.

Item	Inadequate		Minimal		Good		Excellent
	1	2	3	4	5	6	7

Item 2. Reading and writing simple numbers

1.1 Attention is not paid to the reading and writing of simple numbers.

1.2 Posters or written numbers are not displayed in the room.

3.1 Numbers and the equivalent objects are shown next to each other (e.g. the number '3' next to three apples).

3.2 Some children occasionally read and write numbers.

3.3 Children's attention is drawn to number sequence by a number line or verbal interaction.

5.1 Children are encouraged to read and write simple numbers routinely.

5.2 Children have materials available which support them in writing numbers, e.g. wooden numerals or other number shapes.

7.1 There are planned classroom activities containing numbers and adults encourage reading and writing numbers in a variety of materials.

7.2 Written number work is linked to a practical purpose e.g. labelling items in the home corner on a cafe menu or pricing items in a shop corner or putting the birthday number on a birthday card.

Item	Inadequate		Minimal		Good		Excellent
	1	2	3	4	5	6	7

Item 3. Mathematical Activities:

Shape and space (select either Sections 3 or 4 for evidence; choose the one which was most apparent during the observation).

1.1 Shape is rarely commented on in ordinary play or daily routines.

3.1 Some different shapes are available.

3.2 Children's attention is drawn to shape in their environment, e.g. round balls, square windows.

3.3 Shape is an explicit part of some activities indoors.

5.1 A wide variety of shapes are available and adults draw children's attention to specific shape names, e.g. circle, square, triangle, rectangle.

5.2 Staff draw children's attention to shape in the children's own work e.g. drawings, models.

7.1 Many activities and materials are available which encourage children to **generalise** shape across a variety of contexts, e.g. art activities, construction activities, group play arrangements, role-play.

7.2 Activities develop and extend concepts beyond basic shapes and colours e.g. to include properties of two or three dimensional shapes.

7.3 Staff encourage children to understand the properties of different shapes, e.g. 3 sides of a triangle, and to use this understanding to solve shape puzzles and to apply their knowledge to new situations.

7.4 Staff plan activities which demonstrate tessellation in shapes.

Item	Inadequate		Minimal		Good		Excellent
	1	2	3	4	5	6	7

Item 4. Mathematical Activities: Sorting, matching and comparing

1.1 Children are not encouraged to sort, match or compare objects and materials e.g. leaves, water containers, construction kit components.

3.1 Some sorting and matching items are available.

3.2 Children sort and/or match by at least one criterion, e.g. heavy/light or by colour only.

3.3 Staff discuss and demonstrate sorting, comparing or matching and allow the children to participate.

5.1 Activities occur regularly which develop and extend sorting and matching skills, using objects in the child's everyday environment.

5.2 Characteristics which form the basis for sorting and matching are made explicit by the adults, e.g. pointed ends on triangles.

5.3 Staff encourage children to use comparative language when matching, comparing or measuring, e.g. big, bigger, biggest, bigger/smaller.

7.1 Children are encouraged to identify the characteristics of sets of objects, e.g. to explain why a set of shapes is alike, saying 'They are all circles'.

7.2 Language which explores sorting, comparing or matching is used in a variety of contexts across a range of activities, e.g. ordering the size of the three bears; this is curlier, bigger, heavier etc. than that.

7.3 Children are encouraged to complete a sorting, matching or comparing activity then repeat using a different criterion, including their own, as the basis for sorting etc., e.g. arrange hats by size, then by shape.

Item	Inadequate		Minimal		Good		Excellent
	1	2	3	4	5	6	7

Science and Environment: N.B. Items 1 and 2 *MUST* be assessed. After assessing Items 1 and 2 you may then select *EITHER* Item 3 or Item 4 or Item 5 for evidence. You may choose the Item that is most apparent during the observation. This science subscale may require access to planning documents.

Item 1. Natural materials

1.1 There is little access indoors to natural materials. e.g.. plants, rocks, pebbles, fir cones.

3.1 Some natural materials are available to the children indoors.

5.1 Natural materials are used beyond decoration to illustrate specific concepts, e.g. growth – planting seeds or bulbs.

7.1 Children are encouraged to identify and explore a wide range of natural phenomena in their environment outside the centre and talk about/describe them.

3.2 Natural materials are accessible outdoors, e.g. plants.

5.2 Through regular activities, children are encouraged to explore the characteristics of natural material, e.g. things that are smooth or rough.

7.2 Children are encouraged to bring natural objects into the centre.

5.3 Adults show appreciation, curiosity and respect for nature when with children, e.g. curiosity and interest rather than fear or disgust about fungi, insects, worms, etc.

7.3 Children are encouraged to make close observations of natural objects and/or draw them.

Item	Inadequate		Minimal		Good		Excellent
	1	2	3	4	5	6	7

Item 2. Areas featuring science/science resources

1.1 The classroom has no area featuring science.

3.1 Science provision includes a selection of items, e.g. some magnets.

3.2 Displays show evidence of seasonal change, e.g. pictures of spring, winter, autumn, summer.

3.3 Pictures/posters are displayed which could be used to generate discussion about science in the world around us, e.g. posters of the body, life cycle of a butterfly.

5.1 A variety of science equipment is readily available for children to use, e.g. hand lenses.

5.2 There is evidence of collections of things with similar and/or different properties, e.g. things that roll, stretch, bounce, are made of plastic, of metal.

5.3 Print resources go beyond story books to some reference books or material on science topics.

7.1 A wide range of science equipment is available e.g. as in 5.1 + tools, mirrors, magnets.

7.2 A range of reference materials is available including books, pictures, charts and photographs etc.

7.3 A large and stimulating science area is set up for the children to use daily.

7.4 Science materials feature in other areas of the centre as well as the one set aside for science.

Item	Inadequate		Minimal		Good		Excellent
	1	2	3	4	5	6	7

Item 3. +Science Activities: Science processes: non-living

Select one of Sections 3 or 4 or 5 for evidence; (choose the one most apparent during the observation, include floating, sinking, melting, evaporation, temperature, heat, pressure, volume, flexibility, hardness, why/how things move.)

In order to assess this you must have observed staff interacting with children at the water trough/sand or other activity area. For higher levels evidence is being sought for engagement with children in scientific processes i.e. close observation, raising questions/making guesses (hypothesising), experimenting (see what happens) and communicating and interpreting results (why has this happened).

1.1 Children are not encouraged to engage in exploring aspects of their physical environment and scientific words and concepts (see 3.2 for examples) do not feature in discussions

3.1 Some science exploration or experiments are carried out by adults, e.g. include deliberate manipulation by adults or children in order to observe the results, e.g. ice cubes put out in sun.

3.2 Scientific words and concepts may be included superficially in activities and are named, e.g. include floating, sinking, melting, evaporation, temperature, heat, pressure, volume, flexibility, hardness, why/how things move.

5.1 Scientific concepts are introduced and children handle materials, e.g. how materials change, what are their features when viewed through magnifying glasses, magnets, sinkers and floaters, etc.

5.2 Adults draw attention to characteristics and changes in materials, e.g. birthday, candles melting.

5.3 Children are encouraged to use more than one sense, e.g. touch, smell, to explore non-living phenomena and talk about their experience.

7.1 Children are encouraged to experience a range of scientific concepts, e.g. upthrust, force, dissolving in water, sand and cookery.

7.2 Adults support children in systematically seeking answers.

7.3 All children have hands-on experience in varied science activities.

7.4 Adults engage the children in discussion about materials and their characteristics and encourage children to ask questions and record results

27

Item	Inadequate		Minimal		Good		Excellent
	1	2	3	4	5	6	7

Item 4. +Science Activities: Science processes: living processes and the world around us

In order to assess this you must have observed staff interacting with children and living things. For higher levels evidence is being sought for engagement with children in scientific processes i.e. close observation, raising questions/making guesses (hypothesising), experimenting (see what happens) and communicating and interpreting results (why this has happened).

1.1 Children are not encouraged to engage in exploring aspects of their physical environment, e.g. plant growth, insect habitat, birth of mammals or hatching of birds and scientific words and concepts do not feature in discussions. See 3.1.	3.1 Some exploration or experiments are carried out by adults, e.g. putting ice cubes out in the sun.	5.1 Scientific concepts from the natural world are introduced and briefly discussed, e.g. worms living in the soil.	7.1 Adults engage the children in discussion about both plant and animal worlds and their characteristics.
	3.2 Scientific words and concepts feature occasionally in activities, e.g. plant growth, insect habitat, birth of mammals or hatching of birds.	5.2 Adults draw attention to characteristics and changes in the natural world where appropriate, e.g. the life cycle of a butterfly, the ageing process.	7.2 Adults encourage children to ask questions and record results.
	3.3 There are living things present either indoors or outdoors, e.g. plants, fish, snails etc.	5.3 Children are encouraged to use more than one sense to explore living phenomena and talk about their experience, e.g. touch and smell etc.	7.3 All children have hands-on experience with living things where appropriate.

Item	Inadequate		Minimal		Good		Excellent
	1	2	3	4	5	6	7

Item 5 Science Activities: Science processes: food preparation

In order to assess this you must have observed staff interacting with children. For higher levels, look for evidence of children being engaged in scientific processes i.e. close observation, raising questions/making guesses (hypothesising), experimenting (see what happens) and communicating and interpreting results (why has this happened).

1.1 No preparation of food or drink is undertaken in front of the children.

3.1 Food preparation is undertaken by adults in front of the children.

3.2 Some children can choose to participate in food preparation, but this is random, not planned in advance.

3.3 Staff discuss with the children food that has been prepared by adults, where appropriate, e.g. burnt toast or new biscuits or food brought in by children.

5.1 Food preparation / cooking activities are provided regularly.

5.2 Most of the children have the opportunity to participate in food preparation.

5.3 The staff lead discussion about the food involved and use appropriate terminology, e.g. melt, dissolve.

5.4 Children are encouraged to use more than one sense (feel, smell, taste) to explore raw ingredients.

7.1 A variety of cooking activities in which all children may take part are provided regularly.

7.2 The ingredients are attractive and the end result is edible and appreciated, e.g. eaten by the children, or taken home.

7.3 The staff lead and encourage discussion on the process of food preparation, such as what needs to be done to cause ingredients to set or melt.

7.4 Staff draw attention to changes in food and question children about it, e.g. what did it look like before, what does it look like now, what has happened to it?

Item	Inadequate		Minimal		Good		Excellent
	1	2	3	4	5	6	7

Diversity Item 1: Planning for individual learning needs. Ask to see the records kept on individual children

1.1 All children in the setting are offered the same range of materials and activities, rather than having activities matched to their age or aptitude.

3.1 Some additional provision is made in terms of developmental stage, or for individuals or groups with specific needs such as learning support or English language support.

5.1 The range of activities provided enables children of all abilities and from all backgrounds to participate in a satisfying and cognitively demanding way, e.g. showing children the different tasks they can attempt with a toy or game.

7.1 The range of activities provided, together with the organisation of social interaction, enables children of all abilities and backgrounds to participate at an appropriate level in both individual and common tasks, e.g. pairing children of different ages and ability for a certain task.

1.2 If planning occurs it does not take account of specific groups or individuals.

3.2 Some of the planning shows differentiation for particular individuals or groups, e.g. simple peg puzzles up to complex jigsaws, fat paint brushes and watercolour brushes.

5.2 Day to day plans are drawn up with the specific aim of developing activities that will satisfy the needs of each child either individually or as groups.

7.2 Planning sheets identify the role of the adult when working with individuals/pairs/or groups of children. Planning also shows a range of ability levels at which a task or activity may be experienced.

Continued on next page

Item	Inadequate		Minimal		Good		Excellent
	1	2	3	4	5	6	7

1.3 If records are kept, they describe activities rather than the child's response or success in that activity, e.g. ticked checklists or sampling of children's work.

3.3 Children's records indicate some awareness of how individuals have coped with activities, or of the appropriateness of activities, e.g. 'needs bilingual support'; 'could only manage to count to 2'.

5.3 Children are observed regularly, and individual records are kept on their progress in different aspects of their development.

7.3 Children are observed regularly and their progress is recorded and used to inform planning.

3.4 Staff show some awareness of the need to support and recognise children's differences, praising children of all abilities publicly.

5.4 Staff regularly draw children's attention to the difference in people in a positive and sensitive manner.

7.4 Staff regularly draw the attention of the whole group to difference and ability in a positive way, e.g. showing disabled children in a positive light; celebrating bilingual ability.

Item	Inadequate		Minimal		Good		Excellent
	1	2	3	4	5	6	7

Item 2 Gender equity and awareness

1.2 Most books, pictures, dolls and displays portray gender stereotypes.

1.2 The staff ignore or encourage stereotyped gender behaviours, e.g. boys are rarely encouraged to work in the home corner, girls are praised for looking pretty or boys for being strong.

3.1 Some books, pictures and displays include images which do not conform to gender stereotypes, e.g. father looking after baby or female police officer.

3.2 Children's activities and behaviour sometimes cross gender stereotypes, e.g. boys cooking or caring for dolls in the home corner, girls playing outside on large mobile toys.

5.1 Many books, pictures and displays show men and women in non-stereotypical roles e.g. female doctors or plumbers.

5.2 Children are explicitly encouraged to participate in activities which cross gender boundaries, e.g. all children are expected (not forced) to join in construction and gross-motor play.

5.3 Dressing-up clothes encourage non-stereotyped cross-gender roles, girl **and** boy nurse or police outfits and non-gendered clothing e.g. cook's hat/apron, dungarees.

7.1 The children's attention is specifically drawn to books, pictures, dolls and displays that show males and females in non-stereotypical roles and specific activities are developed to help the children discuss gender, e.g. reading and discussing stories like The *Paperbag Princess, Mrs Plug the Plumber* which challenge traditional role-models.

7.2 In encouraging both boys and girls to participate equally in all activities, staff are confident in discussing and challenging the stereotypical behaviours and assumptions of children. Are there specific times when certain things can be done **only** by girls or by boys?

7.3 Male educators are employed to work with children. Where this has not been possible men are sometimes invited to work in the centre with the children.

Item	Inadequate		Minimal		Good		Excellent
	1	2	3	4	5	6	7

Item 3 Race Equality

1.1 Books, pictures, dolls and displays show no or little evidence of ethnic diversity in our society or the wider world.

3.1 The children sometimes play with toys and artefacts from cultures other than the ethnic majority.

3.2 Books, pictures, dolls and displays show people from a variety of ethnic groups even if the images are insensitive or stereotyped, e.g. other nationalities portrayed in national dress, African shown in traditional rural setting, black dolls with white features. .

5.1 Children play with artefacts drawn from an extensive range of cultures, e.g. dressing-up clothes used in dramatic play, cooking and eating utensils. Constant messages that all children do similar everyday things, e.g. go to the park, attend weddings.

5.2 Some books, pictures, dolls and displays show people from a variety of ethnic groups in non-stereotypical roles, e.g. scientists, doctors, engineers.

5.3 Some images / activities show the children that they have much in common with people from other cultural groups, e.g. stress similarities rather than only the differences, e.g. of rituals; also of physical similarities.

5.4 Staff intervene appropriately when child or adult in the setting shows prejudice.

7.1 Staff develop activities with the express purpose of promoting cultural understanding e.g. attention is drawn to similarities and differences in things and people, different cultures are routinely brought into topic work, and visitors and performers reflect a range of cultures.

7.2 Children's attention is specifically drawn to books, pictures, dolls, etc. that show black and ethnic minority people in non-stereotypical roles and familiar situations.

7.3 Specific activities are developed to promote understanding of difference, e.g. paints are mixed to match skin tones to visibly show subtle differences.

7.4 In multi-ethnic areas ethnic minority educators are employed in the centre. Elsewhere, black and ethnic minority people are sometimes invited into the setting to work with the children.

33

Score Sheets

Centre/School_____Date _____

Observer_____ No. staff present_____

No. children enrolled_____ No. children present_____

Age range of children_____ youngest___ oldest. No. children with sp. needs_____

Time observation began_____ Time observation ended_____

Type of disabilities present: Physical/cognitive/social/emotional

LITERACY SUBSCALE

1. Environmental print letters and words 1 2 3 4 5 6 7 Code:_____

Score:_____

	Y N		Y N		Y N		Y N
1.1	☐ ☐	3.1	☐ ☐	5.1	☐ ☐	7.1	☐ ☐
1.2	☐ ☐	3.2	☐ ☐	5.2	☐ ☐	7.2	☐ ☐
		3.3	☐ ☐	5.3	☐ ☐	7.3	☐ ☐

Notes:

2. Book and literacy areas 1 2 3 4 5 6 7 Code:_____

Score:_____

	Y N		Y N		Y N		Y N
1.1	☐ ☐	3.1	☐ ☐	5.1	☐ ☐	7.1	☐ ☐
		3.2	☐ ☐	5.2	☐ ☐	7.2	☐ ☐
						7.3	☐ ☐

Notes:

3. Adult reading with the children 1 2 3 4 5 6 7 Code:_____

	Y N		Y N		Y N		Y N
1.1	☐ ☐	3.1	☐ ☐	5.1	☐ ☐	7.1	☐ ☐
		3.2	☐ ☐	5.2	☐ ☐	7.2	☐ ☐
						7.3	☐ ☐

Score:_____

Notes:

4. Sounds in words 1 2 3 4 5 6 7 Code:_____

Score:_____

	Y N		Y N		Y N		Y N
1.1	☐ ☐	3.1	☐ ☐	5.1	☐ ☐	7.1	☐ ☐
		3.2	☐ ☐	5.2	☐ ☐	7.2	☐ ☐

Notes:

5. Emergent writing/ mark making 1 2 3 4 5 6 7 Code:_____

	Y N		Y N		Y N		Y N
1.1	☐ ☐	3.1	☐ ☐	5.1	☐ ☐	7.1	☐ ☐
1.2	☐ ☐	3.2	☐ ☐	5.2	☐ ☐	7.2	☐ ☐
						7.3	☐ ☐

Score:_____

Notes:

6. Talking and listening 1 2 3 4 5 6 7 Code:_____

Score:_____

	Y N		Y N		Y N		Y N
1.1	☐ ☐	3.1	☐ ☐	5.1	☐ ☐	7.1	☐ ☐
1.2	☐ ☐	3.2	☐ ☐	5.2	☐ ☐	7.2	☐ ☐
				5.3	☐ ☐		

Notes:

A. Subscale (Items 1-6)   Score_____

B. Number of items scored_____

LITERACY SUBSCALE average score (A÷B)_____

MATHEMATICS SUBSCALE

1. Counting   1   2   3   4   5   6   7   Code:_____

	Y N		Y N NA		Y N		Y N		Score:_____
1.1	☐ ☐	3.1	☐ ☐ ☐	5.1	☐ ☐	7.1	☐ ☐		
1.2	☐ ☐	3.2	☐ ☐ ☐	5.2	☐ ☐	7.2	☐ ☐		
		3.3	☐ ☐ ☐	5.3	☐ ☐	7.3	☐ ☐		
						7.4	☐ ☐		

Notes:

---

2. Reading and writing   1   2   3   4   5   6   7   Code:_____
   simple numbers

                                                    Score:_____

	Y N		Y N		Y N		Y N
1.1	☐ ☐	3.1	☐ ☐	5.1	☐ ☐	7.1	☐ ☐
1.2	☐ ☐	3.2	☐ ☐	5.2	☐ ☐	7.2	☐ ☐
		3.3	☐ ☐				

Notes:

---

3. Shape and space   1   2   3   4   5   6   7   Code:_____

                                                    Score:_____

	Y N		Y N		Y N		Y N
1.1	☐ ☐	3.1	☐ ☐	5.1	☐ ☐	7.1	☐ ☐
		3.2	☐ ☐	5.2	☐ ☐	7.2	☐ ☐
		3.3	☐ ☐			7.3	☐ ☐
						7.4	☐ ☐

Notes:

---

4. Sorting, matching   1   2   3   4   5   6   7   Code:_____
   and comparing

                                                    Score:_____

	Y N		Y N		Y N		Y N
1.1	☐ ☐	3.1	☐ ☐	5.1	☐ ☐	7.1	☐ ☐
		3.2	☐ ☐	5.2	☐ ☐	7.2	☐ ☐
		3.3	☐ ☐	5.3	☐ ☐	7.3	☐ ☐

Notes:

A. Subscale (Items 1-4)   Score_____

B. Number of items scored_____

MATHEMATICS SUBSCALE average score (A÷B)_____

Notes:

35

SCIENCE SUBSCALE
 	
1 . Natural materials 1 2 3 4 5 6 7   Code:_____
 	
  Y N   Y N   Y N   Y N   Score:_____
1.1 ☐ ☐ 3.1 ☐ ☐ 5.1 ☐ ☐ 7.1 ☐ ☐
      3.2 ☐ ☐ 5.2 ☐ ☐ 7.2 ☐ ☐
            5.3 ☐ ☐ 7.3 ☐ ☐
 	
Notes:
		3. Science processes: 1 2 3 4 5 6 7 Code:_____
		  Non Living
		  Y N Y N Y N Y N Score:_____
		1.1 ☐ ☐ 3.1 ☐ ☐ 5.1 ☐ ☐ 7.1 ☐ ☐
		      3.2 ☐ ☐ 5.2 ☐ ☐ 7.2 ☐ ☐
		            5.3 ☐ ☐ 7.3 ☐ ☐
		                  7.4 ☐ ☐
		
		Notes:

2. Science   1 2 3 4 5 6 7   Code:_____
  resourcing
  Y N   Y N   Y N   Y N   Score:_____
1.1 ☐ ☐ 3.1 ☐ ☐ 5.1 ☐ ☐ 7.1 ☐ ☐
      3.2 ☐ ☐ 5.2 ☐ ☐ 7.2 ☐ ☐
      3.3 ☐ ☐ 5.3 ☐ ☐ 7.3 ☐ ☐
                  7.4 ☐ ☐
 	
Notes:
		4. Science processes: 1 2 3 4 5 6 7 Code:_____
		  Living processes
		  Y N Y N Y N Y N Score:_____
		1.1 ☐ ☐ 3.1 ☐ ☐ 5.1 ☐ ☐ 7.1 ☐ ☐
		      3.2 ☐ ☐ 5.2 ☐ ☐ 7.2 ☐ ☐
		      3.3 ☐ ☐ 5.3 ☐ ☐ 7.3 ☐ ☐
		
		Notes:

3. +Science processes: 1 2 3 4 5 6 7   Code:_____
  Non Living
  Y N   Y N   Y N   Y N   Score:_____
1.1 ☐ ☐ 3.1 ☐ ☐ 5.1 ☐ ☐ 7.1 ☐ ☐
      3.2 ☐ ☐ 5.2 ☐ ☐ 7.2 ☐ ☐
            5.3 ☐ ☐ 7.3 ☐ ☐
                  7.4 ☐ ☐
 	
Notes:
		5. Science processes: 1 2 3 4 5 6 7 Code:_____
		  Food preparation
		  Y N Y N Y N Y N Score:_____
		1.1 ☐ ☐ 3.1 ☐ ☐ 5.1 ☐ ☐ 7.1 ☐ ☐
		      3.2 ☐ ☐ 5.2 ☐ ☐ 7.2 ☐ ☐
		      3.3 ☐ ☐ 5.3 ☐ ☐ 7.3 ☐ ☐
		            5.4 ☐ ☐ 7.4 ☐ ☐
		
		Notes:

A. Subscale (Items 1-5)   Score_____

B. Number of items scored_____

SCIENCE AND ENVIRONMENT average score (A÷B)_____

---

3. Race Equality 1   2   3   4   5   6   7   Code:_____

	Y N		Y N		Y N		Y N	Score:_____
1.1	☐ ☐	3.1	☐ ☐	5.1	☐ ☐	7.1	☐ ☐	
		3.2	☐ ☐	5.2	☐ ☐	7.2	☐ ☐	
				5.3	☐ ☐	7.3	☐ ☐	
				5.4	☐ ☐	7.4	☐ ☐	

Notes:

DIVERSITY SUBSCALE

1. Individual learning 1   2   3   4   5   6   7   Code:_____
   needs

	Y N		Y N		Y N		Y N	Score:_____
1.1	☐ ☐	3.1	☐ ☐	5.1	☐ ☐	7.1	☐ ☐	
1.2	☐ ☐	3.2	☐ ☐	5.2	☐ ☐	7.2	☐ ☐	
1.3	☐ ☐	3.3	☐ ☐	5.3	☐ ☐	7.3	☐ ☐	
		3.4	☐ ☐	5.4	☐ ☐	7.4	☐ ☐	

Notes:

A. Subscale (Items 1-3)   Score_____

B. Number of items scored_____

DIVERSITY SUBSCALE average score (A÷B)_____

---

2. Gender equity   1   2   3   4   5   6   7   Code:_____

	Y N		Y N		Y N		Y N	Score:_____
1.1	☐ ☐	3.1	☐ ☐	5.1	☐ ☐	7.1	☐ ☐	
1.2	☐ ☐	3.2	☐ ☐	5.2	☐ ☐	7.2	☐ ☐	
				5.3	☐ ☐	7.3	☐ ☐	

Notes:

TOTAL AND AVERAGE SCORE

	Score	Items scored	Av. score
Literacy subscale	_____	_____	_____
Mathematics	_____	_____	_____
Science and environment	_____	_____	_____
Diversity	_____	_____	_____

ECERS-E Profile

Centre/ School _____

Observer 1 (date)_____

Observer 1_____

Teacher/Classroom_____

Observer 2 (date)_____

Observer 2_____

	1	2	3	4	5	6	7	
1. Environmental print								Language Subscale
2 Book and literacy areas								Average Subscale Score
3 Adult reading with child								Observer 1 =
4 Sounds in words								Observer 2 =
5 Emergent writing								
6 Talking and listening								
1 Counting								Mathematics Subscale
2 Reading and writing numbers								Average Subscale Score
3 Shape and space								Observer 1 =
4 Matching, sorting and comparing								Observer 2 =
1 Natural materials								Science Subscale
2 Science resources								Average Subscale Score
3 Non-living								Observer 1 =
4 Living								Observer 2 =
5 Food preparation								
1 Planning for individual needs								Equity - Average Subscale Score
2 Gender equity								Observer 1 =
3 Race equality								Observer 2 =

Appendix A: Overview of the Subscales and Items of the ECERS-R

Space and Furnishings

1	Indoor space
2	Furniture and routine care, play and learning
3	Furnishing for relaxation and comfort
4	Room arrangement for play
5	Space for privacy
6	Child-related display
7	Space for gross motor play
8	Gross motor equipment

Personal care routines

9	Greeting/departing
10	Meals/snacks
11	Nap/rest
12	Toileting/diapering
13	Health practices
14	Safety practices

Language – Reasoning

15	Books and pictures
16	Encouraging children to communicate
17	Using language to develop reasoning skills
18	Informal use of language

Activities

19	Fine motor
20	Art
21	Music/movement
22	Blocks
23	Sand/water
24	Dramatic play
25	Nature/science
26	Math/number

27	Use of TV, video and/or computers
28	Promoting acceptance of diversity

Interaction

29	Supervision of gross motor activities
30	General supervision of children (other than gross motor)
31	Discipline
32	Staff-child interactions
33	Interactions among children

Programme Structure

34	Schedule
35	Free play
36	Group time
37	Provision for children with disabilities

Parents and Staff

38	Provision for parents
39	Provision for personal needs of staff
40	Provision for professional needs of staff
41	Staff interaction an cooperation
42	Supervision and evaluation of staff
43	Opportunities for professional growth

Appendix B
How reliable and valid are the ECERS-R and ECERS-E scales?

I. Reliability and Validity of ECERS-R

ECERS-R is a revision of the well-known and established original ECERS scale. It maintains the same conceptual framework as well as the same basic scoring approach and administration. Since the original version has a long history of research and demonstrating that quality as measured by the ECERS has good predictive validity (Peisner-Feinberg and Burchinal, 1997; Whitebook, Howes and Phillips, 1989) the revised version was expected to maintain that form of validity. However, research on the revised instrument reported here indicates predictive validity.

Have the changes to the scale affected the inter-rater reliability? An extensive set of field tests of the ECERS-R was conducted in the spring and summer of 1997 in 45 classrooms (reported in Sylva *et al* 1999). The authors were not satisfied with the inter-rater reliabilities obtained and decided that further revision was needed. Data from the first exercise were used to determine changes needed to obtain a fully reliable instrument. Substantial revisions were made to the first field-test draft of the scale, using the indicator-level reliabilities as a guide to focus the training process. After the revisions were made, a second test, focusing on inter-rater reliability, was conducted in a sample of 21 classrooms, equally distributed among high-, medium- and low-scoring rooms in the initial test. Even though this test was conservative, with minimal chances to develop reliability through the discussions that customarily take place following a practice observation, the results of the second test were quite satisfactory.

Overall, the ECERS-R is reliable at the indicator and item level, and at the level of the total score. The percentage of agreement across the full 470 indicators in the scale is 86.1%, with no item having an indicator agreement level below 70%. At the item level, the proportion of agreement was 48% for exact agreement and 71% for agreement over one point. Perhaps the most appropriate measure of reliability on a scale such as the ECERS is the Kappa, which takes into account the distance between scores given by two independent raters, rather than simple agreement or non-agreement. Kappas of 0.50 and higher are considered acceptable. All the inter-rater weighted Kappas had scores over .50; most were much higher. Only Item 17, Using language to develop reasoning skills, had a Kappa in the low range. For the entire scale, the correlations between the two observers were .92 product moment correlation (Pearson) and .865 rank order (Spearman). The interclass correlation was .92. These figures are all within the generally accepted range, with the total levels of agreement being quite high. These overall figures are comparable with the levels of agreement in the original ECERS.

Internal consistency of the scale at the subscale and total score levels was also examined. Subscale internal consistencies range from .71 to .88 with a total scale interval consistency of .92. These levels of internal consistency indicate that the subscales and total scale can be considered to form reasonable levels of internal agreement providing support for them as separate constructs.

However, many questions regarding reliability and validity remain unanswered because there have not been enough studies to establish the psychometric properties of ECERS-R. Some of the most recent studies have reported inter-rater reliability figures but no other reliability measurements have been taken (such as test-retest or internal consistency measurements). A study in Philadelphia (Jaeger and Funk, 2001) on the quality of child care reports mean inter-rater reliability .92 (.87 to .97) and mean percent agreement within one rating point 93.5% (83% to 100%). A similar mean percent agreement within one rating point (91.1%) is also reported by another study in Connecticut (Gilliam, 2000) while other researchers managed to establish an overall inter-rater agreement of 84% on the ECERS-R before the start of data collection (de Kruif, McWilliam, Ridley and Wakely, 2000). In summary, the field tests in the US revealed acceptable levels of inter-rater agreement at the three levels of scoring-indicators, items and total score. In addition, there is support for using the scores of the sub-scales and the total score to represent meaningful aspects of the environment.

Moreover the validity of ECERS-R has not been fully established independently of ECERS; that is most researchers anticipate ECERS-R to maintain the good validity characteristics that the ECERS has already demonstrated. Studies will be required to answer questions such as: To what degree does the revised version maintain the same magnitude of score as the original version? And do the two versions both predict child development outcomes similarly?

The EPPE study validated the use of ECERS-R for the UK (Sammons, Sylva, Melhuish, Siraj-Blatchford, Taggart and Elliot, 2002). Based on data from 141 centres, the ECERS-R was associated with the Caregiver Interaction Scale (CIS), which is also a measure of setting quality, to provide information on the construct validity of the ECERS-R. Significant moderate correlations were found between the average total ECERS-R score and two subscales of the CIS (r.58 for the Positive Relationship subscale and r:-.49 for the Detachment subscale). The other two subscales of CIS, Punitiveness and Permissiveness, were also significantly correlated to ECERS-R total in the expected direction: -.23 and -.33 respectively. Especially strong were the correlations between the ECERS-R subscales language and reasoning and social interaction and the CIS subscales positive relationship and detachment (from .48 to .68).

Furthermore, the same study examined the predictive validity of the ECERS-R in relation to cognitive and behavioural outcomes of 3,000 children in a national study (Sammons et al., 2002; Sammons, Sylva, Melhuish, Siraj-Blatchford, Taggart and Elliot, in press). Children's cognitive progress was assessed with the British Ability Scales (BAS II; Elliott, Smith and McCulloch, 1996) administered when the children entered preschool and when the children entered primary school (at the beginning of reception class). The social and behavioural development was assessed by the Adaptive Social and Behaviour Inventory (Hogan, Scott and Baurer, 1992). The ECERS-R, either as a total score or a subscale score, was not related to cognitive progress on a number of measures (pre-reading, early number concepts, language, non-verbal reasoning and spatial awareness/reasoning), controlling for a wide range of child, parent, family, home and other pre-school characteristics. The only statistically significant positive effect was associated with the social interaction subscale and the early number concepts. However, there were several significant associations between the ECERS-R and the behavioural development measures. There was a significant positive effect associated with the co-operation and conformity subscale and a) the ECERS-R average total, b) the language and reasoning subscale, and c) the social interaction subscale. This last subscale was also positively associated with children's independence and concentration.

As for the factor structure of ECERS-R, although there has not yet been a confirmatory factor analysis to support the item and subscale structure and content of the instrument, two studies have conducted principal components analysis to identify the underlying dimensions that explain the scores in the ECERS-R.

Holloway and her colleagues (2001) used data collected from 92 centres. Their analysis came up with 12 (out of 42 items) principal components with an eigenvalue larger than one. Subsequent analyses with rotation suggested the use of just the first principal component which explained 25.57% of the total variance. The items that loaded on this first component were quite variable, mainly representing the dimensions of space, materials and interactions. The results are not consistent with previous research on the original ECERS which usually has provided two factors, one focusing on the teaching aspect of environments and one on the provision of opportunities aspect (Rossbach, Clifford and Harms, 1991; Whitebook, Howes and Phillips, 1989).

Principal components analysis conducted by Sylva and her colleagues (1999) on the 141 centres of the EPPE study resulted in a two-factor solution for the ECERS-R; the first factor is called Activities and Facilities and accounts for over 30% of the variance. The second factor is Communication and Supervision and can explain 7% of the variance in the scores. The analysis ended up with 11 factors that had an eigenvalue larger than one, but the first two were clearly standing out from the rest, explaining together about 38% of the total variance. The items that loaded more strongly on these two factors can be seen in Table 1.

Table 1 ECERS-R items with the higher loadings on the two factors

Factor 1	Loading	Factor 2	Loading
Sand/Water	0.762	General supervision of children	0.816
Opportunities for personal growth	0.736	Discipline	0.807
Art	0.724	Staff-child interactions	0.742
Child related displays	0.711	Informal use of language	0.741
Blocks	0.656	Language to develop reasoning skills	0.661
Provision for professional needs for staff	0.619	Interactions among children	0.645
Provision for personal needs for staff	0.608		

Clearly, the two-factor solution of the EPPE analysis is closer to the factor structure found in ECERS. Clifford and his colleagues (1998) conducted a confirmatory factor analysis on the ECERS using data obtained from the US, Germany, Portugal and Spain. They confirmed the presence of two factors: the first is called Teaching and Interaction and is very similar to the second factor of the EPPE study, and the other is called Space and Materials and closely resembles the first factor of the EPPE study. In both studies internal consistency in each factor was very high, around .9.

In addition, larger data sets will be required to examine empirically the factor structure of the scale. Further research will be needed to determine the extent to which the ECERS-R reveals the same empirical dimensions as the original ECERS. Before turning to reliability and validity of ECERS-E, there follows a brief summary of important studies using the previous version of ECERS.

Previous studies using the former ECERS (before revision to ECERs-R)

Many studies all over the world have used the ECERS to describe education and care processes (Farquhar, 1989; Hagekull and Bohlin, 1995; Lera, Owen and Moss, 1996; Rossbach, Clifford and Harms, 1991; Scarr, Eisenberg and Deter-Deckard, 1994; Tietze, Cryer, Bairrao, Palacios and Wetzel, 1996; and Whitebook, Howes and Pillips, 1989). In all the various countries where the scale has been used, it has proven to be reliable and valid with minor adaptations, suggesting that children from various background 'require similar inputs for success in developmental areas valued in western industrialized countries' (Harms, Clifford and Cryer, 2002). A further group of studies have demonstrated that the quality characteristics measured in ECERS are significantly related to children's developmental outcomes (Beller, Stahnke, Butz, Stahl and Wessles, 1996; Cost, Quality and Child Outcomes in Child Care Centre Research Team, 1995; Kwan, Sylva and Reeves, 1998: Kwan, 1997; McCartney, 1984; Peisner-Feinberg and Burchinal, 1997; Phillips, Scarr and McCartney, 1987; Phillips, McCartney and Scarr, 1987).

II. Reliability and validity of ECERS-E

In the Sylva *et al.* study (1999) the relationship between ECERS-R and ECERS-E was also examined. The correlation coefficient was 0.78 indicating a strong positive relationship between the two measures. Even though the two instruments focus on different dimensions of the pre-school settings, they both measure a general construct of 'quality'. Therefore, it is expected that centres obtaining a high score on the ECERS-R will also obtain a high score on the ECERS-E.

Inter-rater reliability on the ECERS-E was calculated from data obtained from the same 25 randomly chosen centres that were also used in the reliability analysis of the ECERS-R (Sylva *et al.*,1999). The reliability coefficients were calculated separately for separate regions, both percentages of exact agreement between the raters and as a weighted kappa coefficient. The percentages of inter-rater agreement range from 88.4 to 97.6 and the kappas range from 0.83 to 0.97, indicating very high levels of agreement between raters.

Factor analysis conducted on the ECERS-E in 141 centres (Sylva *et al.*, 1999) indicated the presence of two factors that together account for about 50% of the total variance in the scores. The first factor is called Curriculum Areas and the second is called Diversity. Table 2 presents the items that load more strongly (higher than .6) on these two factors.

Table 2 ECERS-E items with the higher loading on the two factors

Factor 1	Loading	Factor 2	Loading
Environmental print letters and words	0.684	Gender equity	0.763
Natural materials	0.683	Race equality	0.702
Counting	0.678	Book and literacy areas	0.643
Science resourcing	0.656	Talking and listening	0.649
Sounds in words	0.634		

Cronbach's alpha was calculated for each factor and for factor 1 was high (0.84) but moderate for factor 2 (0.64). Therefore internal reliability is high only for the first factor, indicating that more factor analyses on the ECERS-E are needed in order to support the factor structure provided by the EPPE study.

Construct and predictive validity of the ECERS-E scale for the UK have been successfully demonstrated by the same study on 141 pre-school settings (Sylva *et al.,* 1999; Sammons *et al.*, 2002; Sammons *et.al.*, in press). Apart from the high correlation between the ECERS-E and the ECERS-R, construct validity of this new scale has also been established through the strong relationship with the CIS, a scale for assessing the relationships between setting staff and children. Sammons and her colleagues (2002) report significant moderate correlations between the ECERS-E average total and Positive Relationship (r:.59) and Detachment (r:.-45), two CIS subscales. All correlations were in the expected direction and the correlation coefficients between all the ECERS-E subscales and the CIS subscales ranged from low to moderate, with the positive relationship subscale being moderately associated with all ECERS-E subscales (from .45 to .58).

The predicative validity of the ECERS-E in relation to cognitive progress was found to be better than the power of ECERS-R in the EPPE study on 3,000 children. Controlling for a large number of child, parent, family, home and pre-school characteristics, the ECERS-E average total was significantly associated in a positive direction with pre-reading scores, early number concepts and non-verbal reasoning. The literacy subscale had a significant positive effect both on pre-reading and on early number concepts. In addition, non-verbal reasoning was significantly affected in a positive direction by the maths subscale of the ECERS-E, the diversity subscale and almost significantly by the science and environment subscale. The diversity subscale had also a significant positive effect on early number concepts. As for the behavioural outcomes, although just missing significance at .05, trends of the average total ECERS-E were positive on two of the measures of social/behavioural development: independence/concentration and co-operation/conformity (Sammons et al., in press).

III Quality across nations and cultures

Quality is not a universal concept but depends on national curricula and cultural priorities. The outcomes deemed important in children's development will relate in different ways to the many measures of quality. If academic achievement is valued at the start of school, then the ECERS-E is a good predictor of children's readiness for school. This readiness includes language, numeracy skill and the component skills of early literacy. But if social outcomes are valued, then the social interaction scale on the ECERS-R may be a better predictor of a child's good start at school. The social outcomes related most to the processes observed in the ECERS-R were children's independence and cooperation/conformity.

Appendix C: Ordering Information
The Effective Provision of Pre-School (EPPE) Project Technical and ECERS-R

Please note that some papers are now into reprints which are slightly more expensive than their original publication price.

Tech. Paper 1 – *An Introduction to the Effective Provision of Pre-school Education* (EPPE) Project ISBN 085473 591 7 Autumn 1999 Price £8.50

Tech. Paper 2 – *Characteristics of the EPPE Project sample at entry to the study* ISBN 085473 592 5 Autumn 1999 Price £4.00

Tech. Paper 3 – Contextualising EPPE Interviews with Local Authority co-ordinators and centre managers ISBN 085473 593 3 Autumn 1999 Price £3.50

Tech. Paper 4 – *Parent, family and child characteristics in relation to type of pre-school and socio-economic differences* ISBN 085473 594 Autumn 1999 Price £4.00

Tech. Paper 5 – *Characteristics of the Centre in the EPPE Study (Interviews)* ISBN 085473 595 X Autumn 2000 Price £5.00

Tech. Paper 6 – *Characteristics of the Centres in the EPPE Sample Observational Profiles* ISBN 085473 596 8 Autumn 1999 Price £8.50

Tech. Paper 6a *Characteristics of Pre-School Environments* ISBN 085473 597 6 Autumn 1999 Price £8.50

Tech. Paper 7 – *Social/behavioural and cognitive development at 3-4 years in relation to family background* ISBN 085473 598 4 Spring 2001 Price £5.00

Tech. Paper 8a – *Measuring the Impact of Pre-School on Children's Cognitive Progress over the Pre-School Period* ISBN 085473 599 Autumn 2002 Price £8.50

Tech. Paper 8b – *Measuring the Impact of Pre-School on Children's Social/Behavioural Progress over the Pre-School Period* ISBN 085473 683 2 Spring 2003 Price £8.50

Tech. Paper 9 – *Report on age 6 assessment* ISBN 085473 600 X Pub. Date: Summer 2003 Price tba

Tech. Paper 10 – *Intensive study of selected centres* ISBN 085473 601 8 Pub. Date: Summer 2003 Price tba

Tech. Paper 11 – *Report on the continuing effects of pre-school education at age 7* ISBN 085473 602 6 Pub. Date: Summer 2003 Price tba

Tech. Paper 12 – *The final report* ISBN 085473 603 4 Pub. Date: Spring 2004 Price tba

Related Publications

The Early Childhood Environment Rating Scale: Revised Edition (1998). Harms, Clifford and Cryer

ISBN 08077 3751 8 Available from Teachers College Press, Columbia University, 1234 Amsterdam Avenue, New York NY10027

Ordering information – For other EPPE Publications

The Bookshop at the Institute of Education. 20, Bedford Way, London WC1H OAL. Tel 00 44 (0) 207 612 6050, Fax 0207 612 6407 e-mail ioe@johnsmith.co.uk website: www.johnsmith.co.uk/ioe or The EPPE Office. The University of London, Institute of Education. 20 Bedford Way, London. WC1H OAL. U.K.Telephone 00 44 (0) 207 612 6219 / Fax. 00 44 (0) 207 612 6230 / e-mail b.taggart@ioe.ac.uk

Please Note: prices will vary according to size of publication and quantities ordered. Visit the EPPE Website on: http://www.ioe.ac.uk/cdl/eppe/

References

Beller, K., Stahnke, M., Butsz, P., Stahl, W. and Wessels, H. (1996). Two measures of the quality of group care for infants and toddlers. *European Journal of Psychology of Education*, 11(2), 151-167.

Clifford, R.M., Burchinal, M.R., Harms, T., Rossbach, H.G. and Lera, M.J. (1998). *Factor structure of the Early Childhood Environment Rating Scale (ECERS): An international comparison.* Chapel Hill, N.C.: Frank Porter Graham Child Development Center.

Cost, Quality and Child Outcomes in Child Care Research Center Research Team (1995). *Cost, quality and child outcomes in child care settings: Public Report.* Denver: Department of Economics, Center for Research and Social Policy, University of Colorado at Denver.

De Kruif, R.E.L., McWilliam, R.A., Ridley, S.M. and Wakely, M.B. (2000). Classification of teachers' interaction behaviours in early childhood classrooms [Electronic version]. *Early Childhood Research Quarterly*, 15(2), 247-268.

Elliott, C.D., Smith, P.and McCulloch, K. (1996). *British Ability Scales Second Edition.* (BAS II). Windsor, Berks: NFER-Nelson.

Farquhar, S. (1989. Assessing New Zealand child day care quality using the Early Childhood Environment Rating Scale. *Early Childhood Development and Care,* 47, 93-105.

Gilliam, W.S. (2000). *The School Readiness Initiative in South-Central Connecticut: Classroom quality, teacher training, and service provision.* Final Report of findings for fiscal year 1999. Retrieved December 2, 2002 from http://nieer.org/resources/research/CSRI1999.pdf

Hagekull, B.and Bohlin, G. (1995). Day care quality, family and child characteristics and socioemotional development. *Early Childhood Research Quarterly,* 10(4), 505-526.

Harms, T., Clifford, R.M.and Cryer, D. (1998) *Early Childhood Environmental Rating Scale, Revised Edition* (ECERS-R), Teachers College Press.

Harms, T., Clifford, R.M. and Cryer, D. (2002). Introduction to the Harms, Clifford and Cryer Early Childhood Environment Rating Scales. Retrieved December 4, 2002 from http://www.fpg.unc.edu/~ecers/intro_frame.html

Harms, T., Clifford, R.M. and Cryer, D. (2003) *Infant/Toddler Environmental Rating Scale-Revised* (ITERS-R) Teachers College Press.

Harms, T., Jacobs., E.V., and White, D.R. (1996) *School-Age Care Environmental Rating Scale* (SACERS) Teachers College Press.

Hogan, A.E., Scott, K.G.and Baurer, C.R. (1992). The Adaptive Social Behaviour Inventory (ASBI): A new assessment of social competence in high risk three year olds. *Journal of Psychoeducational Assessments*, 10, 230-239.

Holloway, S.D., Kagan, S.L., Fuller, B., Tsou, L. and Carroll, J. (2001). Assessing child-care quality with a telephone interview [Electronic version]. *Early Childhood Research Quarterly,* 16, 165-189.

Jaeger, E.and Funk, S. (2001). *The Philadelphia child care quality study: An examination of quality in selected early education and care settings.* A technical report submitted to the Improving School Readiness project of the united way of southeastern PA. Retrieved December 2, 2002 from http://psych.sju.edu/faculty/Jaeger/JaegerFunk2001.pdf

Kwan, C. (1997). The effects of environmental variations in day care centres on the development of young children in Singapore. PhD Thesis. University of London.

Kwan, C., Sylva, K. and Reeves, B. (1998). Day care quality and child development in Singapore. *Early Child development and Care*, 144, 69-77.

Lera, M.J., Owen, C. and Moss, P. (1996). Quality of educational settings for four-year-old children in England. *European Early Childhood Education Research Journal*, 4(2), 21-33.

McCartney, K., Scarr, S., Phillips, D., Grajek, S. and Schwartz, J.C. (1982). Environmental differences among day care centres and their effects on children's development. In E.F. Ziegler and E.W. Gordon (Eds.), *Day Care: Scientific and Social Policy issues.* Boston, MA: Auburn House.

Melhuish, E.C., (1994). What affects the quality of care in English playgroups? *Early Development and Parenting,* 3(3),135-143.

Peisner-Feinberg, E. and Burchinal, M. (1997). Relations between pre-school children's child care experiences and concurrent development: The Cost, Quality and Outcomes Study. *Merrill Palmer Quarterly*, 43(3), 451-447.

Phillips, D., McCartney, K. and Scarr, S. (1987). Child care quality and children's social development. *Journal of Applied Developmental Psychology,* 23(4), 537-543.

Phillips, D., Scarr, S. and McCartney, K. (1987). Dimensions and effects of child care quality: The Bermuda study. In D. Phillips (Ed.), *Quality in child care: What does research tell us?* NAYEC Monograph Series, vol. 1, Washington, DC: National Association for the Education of Young Children.

QCA (2000), *The Foundation Stage Curriculum Guidance.* London, Qualifications and Curriculum Guidance Association.

Rossbach, H.G., Clifford, R.M. and Harms, T. (1991). *Dimensions of learning environments: cross national validation of the Early Childhood Environment Rating Scale.* Paper presented at the annual meeting of the American Educational Research Association, Chicago, IL.

Sammons, P., Sylva, K., Melhuish, E., Siraj-Blatchford, I., Taggart, B. and Elliot, K. (2002) *Measuring the impact of pre-school on children's cognitive progress over the pre-school period. Technical Paper 8a.* London: Institute of Education.

Sammons, P., Sylva, K., Melhuish, E., Siraj-Blatchford, I., Taggart, B. and Elliot, K. (in press). *Measuring the impact of pre-school on children's social behavioural development over the pre-school period.Technical Paper 8b.* London: Institute of Education.

Scarr, S., Eisenberg, M. and Deater-Deckard, K. (1994). Measurement of quality in child care centers. *Early Childhood Research Quarterly,* (9), 131-151.

Siraj-Blatchford, I. (2002a) Final annual evaluation report of the Gamesley Early Excellence Centre. Unpublished report, London, Institute of Education.

Siraj-Blatchford, I. (2002b) Final annual evaluation report of the Thomas Coram Early Excellence Centre. Unpublished report, London, Institute of Education.

Swaminathan, M. *et al.* (2000) *The Tamil Nadu Early Childhood Environmental Rating Scale (TECERS)*, Chennai, India, M.S. Swaminathan Research Foundation.

Sylva, K., Siraj-Blatchford, I., Melhuish, E., Sammons, P., Taggart, B., Evans, E., Dobson, A., Jeavons, M., Lewis, K., Morahan, M. and Sadler, S. (1999). *Characteristics of the centres in the EPPE sample: Observational profiles. Technical Paper 6.* London: Institute of Education.

Sylva, K. (2001). Adapting the Early Childhood Environment Rating Scale (ECERS) to Other Countries and Cultures. Paper presented at the 82nd Annual Meeting of the American Educational Research Association, Seattle.

Tietze, W., Cryer, D., Bairrao, J., Palacios, J., and Wetzel, G. (1996). Comparisons of observed process quality of early child care and education in five countries. *Early Childhood Research Quarterly*, 11(4), 447-475.

Whitebook, M., Howes, C. and Phillips, D. (1989). *Who cares? Child care teachers and the quality of care in America.* Final report on the National Child Care Staffing Study. Oakland, CA: Child Care Employee Project.